AF323260

REMINISCENCES OF A TRIP ACROSS THE
PLAINS IN 1846 AND EARLY DAYS
IN CALIFORNIA

Judge Gallant Duncan Dickenson

Pioneer of 1846 and father-in-law of
Luella Dickenson.

Of this edition seven-hundred-eighty-five copies were printed.

This is Copy Number _______ .

REMINISCENCES OF A TRIP ACROSS THE PLAINS IN 1846 AND EARLY DAYS IN CALIFORNIA

LUELLA DICKENSON

YE GALLEON PRESS

FAIRFIELD, WASHINGTON

1977

The photographs of Peter Burnett and Judge Dickenson, also the old line drawings were furnished by the California State Library, Sacramento.

Library of Congress Cataloging in Publication Data

Dickenson, Luella.

Reminiscences of a trip across the plains in 1849 and early days in California.

Originally published in 1904 by Whitaker & Ray Co., San Francisco.

1. Overland journeys to the Pacific. 2. Pioneers—California—Biography. 3. California—Biography. 4. Indians of North America—the West. I. Title.

F592.D43   1977   978'.03   77-8983

ISBN 0-87770-180-6

ACROSS THE PLAINS IN 1846

TABLE OF CONTENTS

Printing from the workshop of Glen Adams which is located in the pleasant country village of Fairfield, Washington, in southern Spokane County. The offset text printing in brown is by Joseph Coryell. Letterpress printing in bright blue, orange and green is by Glen Adams. The paper stock is Howard Sandstone, felt finish.

Peter H. Burnett

who came out to the Willamette as
a member and organizer of the great
immigration of 1843, and who later
became the first Governor of
California.

ACROSS THE PLAINS IN 1846

The Emigrants.

OR MANY YEARS I have jotted down conversations had with my husband in reference to his trip across the plains, and early days in California. Nothing has given me more pleasure than his reminiscences. He left Independence, Missouri, with his parents and five other children, at that being fifteen years old.

A party of emigrants consisting of five hundred people, with one hundred wagons drawn by oxen (horses and mules were not used as the Indians would have stolen them), met at the rendezvous, choosing his father, G. D. Dickenson, Captain of the company.

May 1st. 1846, was the day set for them to start. Friends came from far and near to say farewell, never expecting to hear from them again. It was the Captain's duty to travel ahead during the latter part of each day for the purpose of selecting camping grounds. Wood, water and grass could not always be obtained at the same place. Finding water, he would return in time to fill all their kegs to supply them during the night.

Many were induced to cross the plains to regain their health. Among the invalids were Mr. Hicklen and his wife, who were consumptives. They had two children, the elder a girl about two years old, the other a baby boy, hardly able to sit alone. One evening having struck camp, and whilst at supper, it was announced that Mr. Hicklen and his wife had passed away, she dying five minutes later than her husband.

The next morning a grave was dug in the road, in which they were placed side by side, wrapt in blankets. First, brush was thrown over them, then dirt shoveled in until filled, when it was made as smooth as possible. On resuming their journey the teams and loose stock were driven over the grave that all signs might be obliterated, to prevent the Indians disinterring the bodies for their clothing, which was their custom. The babies, Mary and Jimmy, were cared for in turns by the company all the way over.

My husband, not realizing the treachery of the Indians, had many hair-breadth escapes. One night he was placed upon picket duty some distance from camp. Hearing voices (the moon was shining brightly) he looked down the ravine and saw two Indians between him and the wagons. Creeping towards them unseen, he hesitated whether to shoot or not, thinking if they went in a different direction he would avoid raising the alarm, which happily they did. At another time he saw something crawling through the grass that looked like a wild animal, but proved to be an Indian disguised in a wolf skin, in order to slip through the guard and reach the few horses that were used for the saddle. If they succeeded in getting through they would secure some of the horses and raise the Indian yell to frighten the others, so as to make them break loose. Once outside the pickets they would always get away with them. He was sitting on the ground with his rifle half cocked, ready for any emergency. Upon rising, the Indians observed him and ran half bent in a zig-zag direction, which they do to prevent them from being shot. Giving the alarm the guard was increased for the rest of the night.

One more day's journey to the Platte River, where they decided to rest three or four days, wood, water, and grass being plentiful. It was dark when they arrived; however, they managed to make all the arrangements necessary for the night with little trouble.

The next morning great herds of buffalo were seen in the distance. Soon after breakfast a party of hunters, composed of Henry Smith, Peter Quivy, and a man named Hannah, with two others whose names could not be recalled, including my husband, who accompanied them to hold their horses when they dismounted, started out in the direction of the mountains. Band after band of antelope were seen. Sometimes they came near enough for one to see their eyes, then they would wheel and go in another direction; but they were not molested, as buffalo were preferred.

When about eight miles from camp, they saw a buffalo upon a knoll, two or three hundred yards ahead. Dismounting, they crept cautiously towards it. Suddenly the report of rifles was heard. The buffalo raised his head, sniffed the air, and disappeared on the other side. The hunters followed on foot. The day was intensely warm, and their canteens of water had been forgotten. After waiting some time, my husband concluded to go as far as the ridge, where he found the buffalo lying dead, and none of the party in sight. Being convinced they had encountered Indians, he mounted the fleetest horse, that he might be ready for a dash to camp should they appear. Greatly to his relief, one of the men came back, saying the others would return in a short time. They returned nearly famished for water, while some could hardly speak.

It was decided to go to the nearest point on the river, which was indicated by the brush that grew upon its banks. Each had killed a buffalo. Beginning on the nearest, they cut out the tenderloin, tying it on a mule brought for the purpose, then continued to the next, two miles farther; and so on to the last, when it was found the mule had all he could carry. Two hours through the scorching sun brought them to the river. Nearly famished, they almost fell from their horses in their anxiety to reach the stream. Lying with their faces in the river they drank until out of breath, then drank again. Mr. Quivy, after drinking himself out of breath the second time, raised up and said, "Be careful, don't drink too much, or you might kill yourselves!" Of course the laugh went around. The poor animals buried their heads to their eyes in the water, seeming to enjoy it even more than their masters.

After refreshing themselves they turned towards camp, reaching there at eight o'clock in the evening. Everybody was alarmed, thinking they had met Indians and had been killed; or had perished for want of water. Morning came only too soon for tired limbs to turn out.

During the night the Indians had collected almost within shooting distance of the pickets, causing them some uneasiness as it portended an attack. All the fighting men were called together to be in readiness. Finally the Chief advanced with a white flag. He was very tall and ferocious looking, wrapped in a blanket of many colors, with a headdress of feathers, and moccasins upon his feet. The Captain went to meet him. He said the squaws were loaded down with buffalo skins they wanted to trade for tobac and beads. Only the Chief and five or six Indians besides the squaws were allowed to approach the wagons, as little confidence could be placed in their manifestations of friendship. The forethought of the emigrants in supplying themselves with these articles for the purpose of propitiating the Indians no doubt saved them many encounters. When the trading was finished they were escorted back and soon were out of sight.

The Captain was often invited to smoke the pipe of peace, but never having tasted tobacco or liquor was not prepared for the occasion. The company had proceeded a short distance on that day when the cry was heard, "The buffalo! The buffalo!" They were dangerous when frightened. Woe to the object that got in their path. They were coming in their direction. Hastily unhitching the oxen, they chained them to the wheels to prevent a stampede. The dust rose in clouds. The rumbling of their hoofs as they struck the plain was like distant thunder. On they came with their heads down and their shaggy eyebrows hanging over their eyes. The emigrants had not more than time to get in the wagons when the buffalo struck the line, knocking down the cattle and jumping over the wagons, endangering the lives of the occupants, who miraculously escaped with only a few bruises.

The company traveled up the Platte River for days in a northwesterly direction. At last they found a fording place a mile at least, from bank to bank. Some of the party were terror-stricken, and insisted on seeking a narrower place. The Captain knew a narrower place would be deeper, so he said he would cross there, and as many as desired could follow. However, to reassure them, he crossed over on horse back and returned. The water was up to the hubs, and at times as high as the beds of the wagons. The teams ahead stirred up the sand, and there being quite a current it shifted, making it still deeper for those following. At times the small stock were compelled to swim. The drivers were obliged to wade to manage their teams, keeping them against the current in order to make the landing on the opposite side. In spite of all their efforts they were beaten down several hundred yards. All rejoiced to arrive safely on terra firma again.

They continued up the river, camping whenever night overtook them, until, reaching a bend in the river, they changed their course to strike the Middle Platte at a point called Fort Laramie. At this point they found a ferryboat made of logs, tied together with ropes made of buffalo hide, on which they crossed their wagons, swimming the stock. The next place was Fort Bridger.

After several weeks' travel they arrived at Soda Springs, where they remained for a few days. The water was enjoyed very much. By adding a little sugar it made a pleasant drink; and for making bread was equal to yeast. From Soda Springs the company went to Fort Hall, a trading post, where they found an adobe house, and a few wigwams. The Mormons, who followly closely, had turned towards Salt Lake.

After several days' rest the emigrants found their way to Mary's River, now called Humboldt, which was reached after several weeks' travel. When they arrived near Battle Mountain, not named at that time, the weather had moderated. However, the days were quite warm, but the nights were cool and pleasant. The rest of the way was exceedingly monotonous, through an alkali plain, until they reached the river, a narrow stream with low banks and brackish water. Here and there a dwarfish tree or shrub could be seen. The company traveled down one side or the other, crossing and recrossing, where they though the road could be improved, until reaching the sink of the river.

Before reaching there, they had great difficulty in keeping the loose stock from being taken by the Indians. At dusk they came quietly on foot, having no horses, and attempting to pass between the rear wagon and those in charge of the stock. The men in charge thought they had managed to prevent their getting any. On striking the camp, owing to the darkness, the stock could not be counted. The next morning, they found quite a number of their work oxen missing, having neglected to chain them to the wheels; also some of their horses and loose stock.

A party of four or five, including my husband, prepared their rifles, supplied themselves with food to last through the day, and went in pursuit, thinking the cattle, being so poor and weak, could be overtaken before reaching the mountains, a distance of twelve or fourteen miles. A short distance from the camp they found one of the work oxen filled with arrows and lying dead. Pushing on with renewed vigor, they reached the base of the mountains, having passed on the journey three or four more oxen that had been killed in the same way. Continuing on the trail some distance up the slope, they finally arrived at the conclusion that it would be dangerous to go farther; and knowing the Indians would kill the cattle when they became too weak to travel, and there would be nothing gained by risking their lives, they retraced their path.

When almost in sight of the camp they saw two objects moving towards them. They soon discovered the objects were two men who had a left a train behind, and were following on to the sink of the river. They were almost famished. The party gave them all the water in their canteens, and told them they would hasten as fast as their jaded animals would carry them and send someone to meet them. When the two men first saw the party they thought they were Indians. The glistening of their rifles in the glaring sunshine relieved them; they then knew the party belonged to the train which they were trying to overtake. One was an Irishman, the other a Dutchman. They were told to follow the trail in the direction the horsemen went. Two men were sent to meet them. When they arrived at camp, supper was ready, of which they partook ravenously, having been many hours without food.

After supper the Dutchman recounted their adventures. He said when they saw the supposed Indians he remarked, "What will we do?" And the Irishman, whose parched tongue would hardly articulate, said, "We will have a d — — dry fight."

Knowing the character of the country they must pass through, and fearing another raid by the Indians, as game in this region was very scarce, the Captain ordered an early start, daylight being so far in advance that the emigrants could hardly see to hitch up their teams. Nothing of note occurred until they reached Hot Springs, where another invalid, Mrs. Hitchcock, died, and was buried in the same manner as the unfortunate Hicklens. The springs were at boiling heat, but a short distance below the stock were able to sip at it.

Almost the hardest day's journey was from this point to the Truckee River. The weather was oppressive, and the poor cattle could hardly drag one foot after the other. Within a short distance of the river, some of them gave out. The emigrants were obliged to double their teams, hitching to just sufficient wagons to haul the women and the children, the men walking. A guard was left to watch the teams.

The Irishman proved to be of great service. It being necessary to send water to the guard, he volunteered to take it to them. Loading himself with the canteens, he journeyed back on foot, risking his life to prove his gratitude for kindness received at their hands. The next evening they got in with the rest of the stock, where a good supper of fresh fish awaited them. Needless to say these were a great treat. The stock, almost perished from hunger, stood in grass to their knees.

The cool atmosphere, clear running stream, and beautiful forest were indeed appreciated by the weary travelers. The camping ground selected was at the point where the railroad crosses the Truckee River today. All were refreshed by their stay at this place, and the stock were beginning to show the effect of the forage, when the company decided to ford the river and proceed on their way.

The Reed and Donner party were a short distance behind. On the way over, they were sometimes ahead; but making a long stay at a camp, Captain Dickenson's party would get in the lead. One of my notes, overlooked, gives an account of Ben Lippencott, who, before reaching the sink of Mary's River, left the camp with a few wagons. The first night out, they were attacked by Indians, and two men, Sally and Burns, were shot with poisoned arrows, which proved fatal. Ben S. Lippencott also received a wound in the calf of his leg. With great presence of mind, he pulled the arrow through, cleansing the wound and making it bleed freely, which saved his life. The party led by Lippencott continued on their journey.

The emigrants reaching the spot where the two men were buried, found a note in the split of a stick, driven in the ground, warning them to beware of the Indians, giving the names of the two men killed.

Up the Truckee Valley.

FTER CROSSING THE TRUCKEE, at the point mentioned, the emigrants continued their journey up the river, which they found very crooked, compelling them to cross very often. One day they crossed fourteen times. Although narrow and not deep, the bowlders in its bed frequently caused the cattle to slip and fall upon their sides, sometimes injuring them. The gorge in average width was only a stone's throw, leaving just enough room for the wagons to pass along the banks of the stream, it being impossible to travel more than two or three miles a day.

About the fifth week, they arrived at a camping ground selected by my husband, where the town of Truckee now stands. Clouds were hanging heavily when they reached there. Captain Dickenson felt anxious, as trappers had told him of the danger of being caught in a snow storm. He had advised the Reed and Donner party to push through at all hazard, as to strike camp meant death. The same snow storm that overtook the Dickenson party, caused the terrible suffering that has been so often told. About 11 A.M. they arrived at a beautiful lake known at present as Donner Lake, the place where the ill-fated Donner party camped. The rain was falling steadily. At any moment it might turn to snow, as the atmosphere was very cold. The emigrants ate their dinner hurriedly, the Captain having gone ahead, as usual, to report the condition of the road. By the time he returned they were ready to start for the summit.

They had not gone far when the snow commenced falling. Such flakes they had never seen. Some declared they were as large as saucers. In a short time the ground was covered, when the snow turned to rain, alternating continually during the ascent. In places deep ravines ran down the sides of the gorge, rendering travel almost impossible. The only way of advancing was to unhitch the oxen and drive them over one at a time. The wheels were taken from the wagon beds, after removing the goods, and all were carried over by the emigrants. The loose stock seemed to realize the danger and did not hurry over the ground. Had they lost their footing they would have rolled down the steep slopes and been dashed to death on the bowlders.

Often trees were found lying across the road. Many of the emigrants could wield the axe. As one would tire another would take his place, so that the obstructions were removed in a short time. Having arrived at a ravine not quite as steep, they would cut down a tree and trim it to the top, leaving the limbs projecting six to eight inches. This they tied to the center of the axle, at the back of the wagons, to serve as a brake, the short limbs plowing ground as they descended. At another place, where it was steeper, they would attach a chain to the back axle, and wind the other end around a tree, so as to unwind slowly as the wagon descended. On the sixth day at dusk, almost exhausted from fatigue and anxiety, the emigrants reached the summit, where they found the snow several inches deep. They struck camp under the beautiful pines that served, to some extent as a shelter, as well as giving them fire and light.

Early the next morning they began the descent. It was still snowing, and heavy black clouds covered the canopy, showing no signs of abatement. The Captain thought it best to travel as fast as possible, feeling that they would be safe when beyond the snow belt. After a few miles of travel the rain began falling, continuing all the way to the valley. During the descent, James Smith, from Kentucky, died, and was buried in the same crude way. He was a devoted friend of my husband, leaving him his clothes, having nothing else to give. His brother-in-law, Mr. Drum, learning that he would join the emigrants, had supplied him with provisions and delicacies to last during the journey. The night Mr. Smith died, my husband sat up with him, giving him water at intervals. About four A.M., tired and worn with hardships he had passed through, he fell asleep. Upon awakening, he found his friend dead. At the time of his death, the company was camping at a place called Ash Hollow, on account of the whitish and sunken appearance of the earth.

Reaching Johnson's cattle ranch on Bear River, the emigrants were invited by the owner to camp there as long as they desired. His hospitality caused them to remain several days. During their stay, Mr. Johnson had a young beef slaughtered, which he presented to them; and also supplied them with a few necessaries, without recompense. He was always held in grateful remembrance. They finally bade adieu to their generous host, and made their way to Sutter's Fort. No settlements were found between the two places. Sacramento Valley at that time was covered with wild oats, bunch grass and clover. The rivers were bordered with trees, but the plains had only a few scattered ones. Thousands of elk could be seen, and some deer that had ventured from the hills.

Sutter's Fort was an adobe building, about thirty feet in length and fifteen in width, having a partition dividing it into two rooms of equal size. The walls were, perhaps, nine feet in height, the roof being covered with tules or tiles. In the center of each room was a cow's hide, upon which was placed the joint of a whale's vertebra, substituted for chairs. Mr. Sutter exceeded his neighbors' generosity in being able to supply the company with a greater quantity of provisions. He farmed an extensive tract of land, hiring Indians to do the work, which gave the place the appearance of a rancheria.

Leaving Sutter's they forded the Mossumnes, Mokelumne and Calaveras Rivers, camping when night overtook them. Reaching a point near the bank of a slough, they struck camp where the city of Stockton now stands. At this place Mr. Campbell, familiarly known as "Uncle Billy," killed an elk. French Camp was the next place, having derived its name from the French hunters having camped there. The following day the company crossed the San Joaquin River a short distance above its mouth. The stream was as clear as crystal, the condition of all California rivers before the discovery of gold, there being no debris. Myriads of fish were seen swimming in the stream. Upon crossing the river, a plain, the continuation of San Joaquin Valley lay before them. It was covered with wild oats upon which thousands of elk, deer, antelope, and wild horses were grazing.

The horses attracted the most attention, being in large bands with a leader that showed remarkable intelligence in managing his band. Sometimes a horse would stray too far from its herd and the leader of another would capture it, driving it into his collection. Then the leader of the band from which the horse was captured would go in pursuit, frequently driving it back. Sometimes the aggressor would try to fight him off. In battle the object of their contentions was forgotten, when it would complacently trot back. Observing this, the combatants would cease fighting, returning to their respective herds.

The Spanish horses were the most graceful animals imaginable, "their colts being perfect models," about fourteen hands in height, usually slender-bodied, with heavy manes and tails which almost swept the ground. All colors were represented, including pinto, an exception to other California horses. The word pinto means spotted, white with intermingled colors, either white and black, white and bay, white and sorrel, or white and bluish gray. To be more explicit, the Americans called them calico horses. Their eyes were often of different colors, one being light blue, called a glass eye, and the other very dark, the eyelashes being white. The nose was invariably Roman, and white at the end, giving it the appearance of not having any hair.

As a rule they were very fractious. The Mexicans call them broncos, often using them for bucking matches, a sport they frequently engaged in.

ACROSS THE PLAINS IN 1846

E HAVE NOW DIGRESSED SOMEWHAT, so we will return to the emigrants. Not far from the foothills, they met Thomas O. Larkin, on his way to Benicia. He was obliged to cross the Sacramento River to get there, making a very roundabout trip, there being no ferries at that date. That night the company camped at a place afterwards called the Mountain House, where a nice cool spring was found. The next camping place was at Robert Livermore's, an Englishman who had married a Spanish woman. Mr. Livermore owned a large band of cattle with an unlimited range. Slaughtering took place once in two or three years, always in the fall, for their hides and tallow, as there was no market for the meat. Each animal gave a profit of about two dollars. The carcass was left lying at the round-up, where they were killed. Indians were employed to render the tallow and care for the hides.

They had a rather crude way of marketing their products. Their wagons consisted of two wooden wheels, from two to three feet in diameter, and a foot thick with a hole in the center to admit the wooden axle, to which a tongue was attached, with a box frame as a wagon bed. The yoke for the cattle was a piece of timber, four or five feet in length, concaved at each end to fit their necks, and lashed securely to their horns with rawhide straps, the tongue being fastened to the center of the yoke with rawhide also. Two Indians were required to drive the team, each supplied with a pole six or eight feet long. One walked behind to prod them up, and the other before to keep them from going too fast. When they wanted them to stop they said "parita."

Another method of carrying tallow was to put it in a hide, to which they attached a riata, taking a turn around the horn of their saddles, and dragging it to market. This latter method was seldom adopted, and only when they had little to carry, and the distance was short.

Mr. Livermore and family lived in a comfortable adobe house, surrounded by a small vineyard. He took great pleasure in placing before the company all that his larder afforded. The next stopping place was a point now known as Pleasanton, where Captain Dickenson lost one of his favorite oxen, it having bogged down in a small marsh. It was found dead the following morning.

The next camping place was San Jose Mission. The first shepherd dog seen by any of the emigrants was near this place, herding a large band of sheep. The Mexicans depended almost entirely upon these dogs to attend to the sheep. The next night they arrived in San Jose, where there were a few adobe houses. Their train was about the first, if not the first, to reach San Jose.

LUELLA DICKENSON

The company stayed in this place several days, then started for Monterey. A short distance from town they met Julius Martin, who told them they would be made prisoners if they went farther, as the Mexicans were organizing their armies in Salinas Valley and Monterey. The company turned back, remaining in Pueblo San Jose, as it was called, several days for the purpose of getting all the families together and deciding where to intrench themselves.

They finally concluded to go to Santa Clara, where there was a deserted street of adobe houses extending one block. The houses proved a safe refuge for the women and children, the walls being so thick it was almost impossible for a rifle ball to pass through. The emigrants first dug a ditch at each end of the street, then topped the willows on the Alameda, making posts, which they placed in the ditch, on end, close together, packing the dirt in well. Next, a pole was secured near the top of the posts with rawhide rope. When finished the fence was about eight feet high. Wagons were placed with the sides against the fence on the inside, and attached to the posts with log chains.

There was some skirmishing during the winter and a few men wounded, not seriously. A company was organized of unmarried men who chose Charles M. Weber as their captain. He had been in California several years, consequently was familiar with the country, and the Spanish language. He was also a good horseman, daring and brave. Although a German, he took an active part in the American cause. Captain Weber's company consisted of fifty or sixty men. Among them were Dan and John Murphy; Jack and Dennis Bennett; and James Dickenson.

The latter part of November, or early in December, 1846, the emigrants intrenched in Santa Clara chose Joseph Aram as their captain. He was a man of commanding appearance, well calculated to be a leader, who had arrived soon after the Dickenson party, April, 1847.

Captain Weber's company went to Yerba Buena (San Francisco) from San Jose, where he had been stationed, to get supplies, and a cannon that was sent around the Horn by the government. Captain Weber anticipated trouble on the way, as the Mexicans were concentrating their forces near the foothills on the west side of the valley, a short distance from Santa Clara. On his return, near Mountain View, he was attacked by two hundred and fifty or three hundred of the enemy, all well mounted. The cannon was a small affair, but every shot told. As the smoke cleared away the Mexicans would make a rush. They were losing heavily, but only one had been wounded in Weber's company, Jack Bennett, not seriously, however.

The Mexican commander concluded to change his tactics by surrounding the wild cattle and driving them through the ranks. The captain was prepared for any movement they might make. When he saw the cattle approaching he waited until they got quite near, then ordered the cannon discharged, which caused them to turn upon the Mexicans in a regular stampede. Such a hurrying and skurrying was never seen before. Weber's company had fought its way down nearly to Santa Clara, where he was re-inforced by Captain Aram's company, who adopted the Indian method of scattering the forces, crouching in the mustard, and giving the Mexicans half of the charges, reserving the rest for closer quarters. The first charge they made three of four of them were unhorsed. Others fell across their horses' necks and were carried off by them. A second charge was made, with the same result. In this charge my husband was run over by a Mexican cavalryman who made a lunge at him with his sabre, failing to reach him. The horse stepped upon his leg, making a serious wound. The war ended March, 1847, peace being declared February, 1848.

One circumstance recalled was of a party given by Mr. Bellamy, who had a Spanish wife. They lived about one hundred yards from the encampment. All the emigrants were invited, but only the young people accepted. Among them were two young married ladies who acted as chaperons. The names of the young ladies who attended were: Miss Pop Allen, afterwards Mrs. Mendenhall; Miss Brown, who married Mr. B. Smith; Miss Margaret Jones, who married Mr. Josiah Beldon; Miss Bennett; Miss Margaret and Miss Lucy Dickenson; Miss Mary Taber, a sufficient number for two sets of the quadrille. My husband and a young man stood guard whilst they danced. It was a beautiful moonlight night. The Mexicans' spurs could be heard rattling and soon they were observed riding through the mustard, taking care not to venture too close. Some doubted Mr. Bellamy's loyalty, which caused the company some anxiety. The dancing continued until almost dawn, when everybody returned, well pleased with the entertainment, which convinced the suspicious of his sincerity.

In May, 1847, G. D. Dickenson and family went to Santa Cruz by way of "Watsonville," as it is now called, there being no wagon road over the mountains. They camped at Soquel, near Mike Lodge's ranch, whose daughter married Thomas Fallon. Like many other Englishmen, Mr. Lodge had married a Mexican lady. Remaining at Soquel two weeks, the family removed to Monterey, at that time a larger place than Yerba Buena (San

Francisco).   Quite a number of enterprising men were found there, among whom were T. O. Larkin, Tolbert H. Bean, Little, a merchant, Gardner, who married a Mexican wife and was afterwards killed by the Indians in San Joaquin valley, David Hartnel, who also married a Mexican wife and had twenty-eight children, Mr. Cooper, father of the late John Cooper, General Nagle, Green Patterson, Curtis, Lovel, Angel, Dr. Amos Isbell, and Taber.

G. D. Dickenson's first thought was to make his family comfortable by building a log house for them to live in until he could complete a more commodious one of brick. The bricks were burned by his two sons, Samuel and William, a man named Marion, Richard Lytton, and Lawrey, the last mentioned being employed to lay the bricks. This was the first brick house built in California, and still stands near the old Custom House.

FIRST BRICK HOUSE IN CALIFORNIA

ACROSS THE PLAINS IN 1846

Gold is Discovered.

FEBRUARY 2, 1848, James W. Marshall and Peter Wemer discovered gold upon land owned by Captain John A. Sutter, of Sutter's Fort, a man who was esteemed by all the officers stationed in California, as well as the emigrants who had been the recipients of his bounty. His lands were practically confiscated by the miners, who camped upon it, and dug it over in their eagerness to find the yellow metal. His cattle and sheep were stolen and his mill rendered useless, as no mill hands could be procured.

The excitement was intense and people from all parts of the Territory hurried to the mines. June 7, 1848, G. D. Dickenson left Monterey, with his family, his destination being Morman Island, on the south fork of the American River. Reaching there they found a few miners and some good diggings. The gold was washed out in a pan by dipping it into the river and continuously shaking it; thereby washing the earth over the edges, leaving the particles of gold in the bottom of the pan. An improvement upon this method was the rocker, made like a cradle. Next came the sluice, which required the overshot wheel to lift the water from the river.

The family remained one month at Mormon Island. Being restless, like others, and thinking the Mokelumne Hill diggings might be better, they went there, where their expectations were realized. The best diggings were in a ravine, afterwards called Dickenson's Gulch. Some of Colonel Stevenson's disbanded soldiers had followed them all the way to this point. They were well meaning, but not of a refined type, being very contentious. They had the greatest respect for Judge Dickenson, depending upon him to settle their disputes. His decisions were always satisfactory; in fact, he was the preserver of the peace. Early in the spring of 1849 the Dickenson family went to Stockton, accompanied by the same disbanded soldiers. On their way they met Colonel Stevenson's party, who had camped the night previous near the Mokelumne River, about twenty-five miles from Mokelumne Hill. During the night their horses strayed away. However they had recovered enough to continue their journey.

Judge Dickenson and his two sons, James and William, had secured three bags of gold dust, the greatest portion of which paid for the construction of the first hotel in Stockton, called the Dickenson House, and capable of accommodating over a hundred guests. The hotel was leased to Messrs. Roach and Mason for thirty thousand dollars a year. It has been claimed that a man named Buzwell erected a log house about 1847, which was called "Buzwell Tavern." As the Dickenson family passed through Stockton, June, 1848, on their way to Monterey from the mines, there were no settlements of any kind; and on their return from Mokelumne Hill there were no houses in the place. Charles M. Weber had landed some goods on the banks of the slough, and had them covered with a canvas tent.

Rev. James Woods in his "California Recollections," states: "Our arrival in Stockton was late on Saturday night. On Sunday morning I sought and found temporary shelter for my family in a kind of boarding house, kept by an old Methodist gentleman who came to California two years previous." The old Methodist gentleman was G. D. Dickenson, at that time Prefect, with the income as mentioned above, who was living in his private residence and through kindness of his heart gave Rev. Woods and family shelter, not temporary, as their stay lasted several weeks, for which Judge Dickenson did not ask or receive a cent.

At that time there were ten or twelve canvas houses, and two or three board shanties. Stockton was the port of the southern mining district. Small vessels discharged their cargoes upon the banks of the slough, being always crowded to their fullest capacity with people bound for the mines. The excitement naturally attracted the lowest element, also, such as gamblers, pickpockets, and burglars. An instance is recalled of a victim of one of this class, a poor washerwoman, who had accumulated three hundred dollars which she had secreted in her canvas house. Whilst engaged in washing at the edge of the slough the money was stolen. Soon discovering her loss, she rushed out of her house, calling upon the citizens to catch the thieves. The bystanders, seeing her distress, went immediately to Judge Dickenson. He and George Belt had their horses saddled, and were soon on their way to overtake the robbers. Irish Mickey and Red Davis, a tall, cadaverous looking fellow, were suspected, as they had disappeared simultaneously. Red Davis was supposed to have committed several murders; also a great many other robberies, having a wide reputation as a horsethief and always eluding his pursuers.

They were found in San Jose. Red Davis had disguised himself as a Mexican. When arrested he was coming from Santa Clara under cover of darkness, and had reached the bridge over the Guadalupe River, on the outskirts of town, when ordered to stop. With an assumed innocence he spoke to his captors in Spanish, asking what was wanted. His hat was pulled down over his eyes, hoping he would not be recognized. The handcuffs were placed upon his wrists and he was then taken to the jail, an old adobe building for the night. The next morning early he was put on a horse, his feet tied together with a rope long enough to enable him to use the stirrups. The horse being led by one, and driven by the other alternately, until they reached Stockon, arriving there, a distance of eighty miles, the same day. Mickey was in jail, having been captured by a posse of citizens.

No time was lost in bringing them to trial. Twelve reputable men were chosen to serve on the jury. A verdict of guilty was rendered and the sentence, as remembered, was passed by Judge Reynolds, that they should be hanged by the neck until dead, two weeks from that time.

Notwithstanding the notorious character of the men, they had their sympathizers. Some of the rough element of Colonel Stevenson's regiment, principally gamblers, had formed themselves into an organization called "The Hounds," for the purpose of defying the laws, and similar to the organization that created the necessity for the Vigilance Committee in San Francisco, resulting in the hanging of Cory and Casey. The leader of the gang, named Ruly, offered to bet ten dollars against a shoestring that neither Mickey nor Davis would be hung.

The situation became alarming. The citizens had armed themselves, ready to carry out the sentence, when a vessel arrived bringing a company of young men, all from New Jersey. They were well armed, and at once volunteered their services. The two men were executed without interference on the part of the Hounds. The execution saved the city a great deal of trouble, besides having a moral effect upon the community. The Hounds disappeared, going to other fields better suited to their calling.

During the administration of Governor Riley, G. D. Dickenson served in the capacity of Prefect. While in office David Terry had some trouble with George W. Belt on account of Dr. Roberts. The trouble originated between Roberts and Belt, which resulted in Roberts challenging Belt, who refused to accept upon the ground of Roberts not being a gentleman. As Roberts' second, Terry asked Belt if he considered him to be a gentleman. Being answered in the affirmative, Terry then took the place of Roberts and Roberts the place of Terry. The duel was to be fought with pistols. The day preceding the one set for the duel, parties appeared before the Prefect, asking that a writ be issued to the sheriff for their arrest. They were placed under arrest and bound over to keep the peace.

LUELLA DICKENSON

In the fall of 1849 Margaret, the elder daughter of Judge Dickenson, married Mr. Lawrey, this being the first wedding in Stockton. About this time rich diggings were found in Sonora. The rush was made from the coast through Pacheco Pass, crossing the ferry established by G. D. Dickenson on the San Joaquin River, near its junction with the Merced. A man named Woods was placed in charge, who was discharged in a short time, and one by the name of Watts took his place. In less than six months the receipts were over four thousand dollars, which he was requested to bring to Stockton. Watts not making his appearance when expected, search was made and his lifeless body found in the house. Not a trace of the murderer or money was ever discovered. It was thought by some that the money had been buried.

Next, came the discovery of the Big and Little Garotes. G. W. Coulter built a hotel near them. He kept an orderly house, and was respected by all who knew him. Quite a settlement grew up which was called Coultersville, as a compliment to the genial landlord. The miners, composed of all grades of humanity, met upon an equal footing. In the evening they assembled in the barroom of the hotel, and would tell stories for each other's amusement. A man named Jim was famous for his improbable stories and possessed the faculty of always extricating himself when cornered.

One story was about an animal found in the hills of Missouri, called the guano, having four feet. On one side, its legs were eight inches longer than those on the other, terminating in sheep hoofs. On the other side were horse hoofs. The head and neck resembled a horse, and the main that of a cow. He was asked how it managed to browse. His answer was, "It feeds around the hill with the long legs on the lower side in order to retain its balance." The next question was, "Should it get frightened and turn around, what would happen?" He replied, "It never gets frightened, but continues to feed around the hill until the top is reached." The next question, "Please tell us how it got down the hill." The reply was, "it rolled down."

Another by the name of Joe told about his sister's wedding. He said that when his sister was preparing for her wedding his family lived away out in the frontier of Vermont. Settlements were few and far between. The minister who performed the ceremony lived twenty miles distant. Two thousand invitations were issued, and the men were sent on horseback to deliver them. Someone remarked, "They must have started several weeks before to deliver so many invitations." He replied, "Oh, no! they only went fifty miles, returning the same day." Some looked incredulous, when he added, "The roads were good and the horses in fine condition; that is, nearly all; but a few were obliged to change horses. The wedding was a grand affair, and cost about ten thousand dollars; but the saddest part of the whole affair was, I fell out the next day with my brother-in-law, and have never spoken to him since." The question was asked, "Joe, what was the trouble about?" "He wanted to pay half the expenses of the wedding, and I wouldn't let him."

How the Mexicans Trained their Horses.

T THIS TIME, lumber was gotten out with a whipsaw, consequently sold at a high figure. Many ceased mining to follow this occupation. The echo of sawing, and rush of water through the sluices; the creaking of the windlass, and dumping of dirt from the shafts, combined with the sighing of the pine trees; and now and then a call of one miner to another, whose voices reverberated through the canyon, made a scene to be remembered.

All commodities were extremely high. A pick sold for fifty dollars; a spade for sixty; a coarse flannel shirt brought twenty-five dollars; boots from sixty to eighty dollars per pair; and shoes twenty to thirty dollars per pair. These prices were seemingly high, until you stop to consider that a miner with pick, pan, and shovel would often take out enough gold in one day's work to pay for all the articles mentioned. Meat sold for one dollar per pound. Some hogs were bought from Mr. Elder near Stockton, and driven to the mines. where they were sold for two hundred and fifty dollars per head. One morning two miners offered three dollars for enough pork for their breakfast, and were sadly disappointed not to get it.

In 1849 San Francisco contained two or three iron houses, and a few frame buildings that had been shipped around Cape Horn. The rest were canvas on frames. Few thought of going there without bags of gold dust. Gambling was carried on extensively, and nearly everybody frequented the gambling houses. However only a small percentage engaged in the games. Many went for the purpose of obtaining information in reference to mining localities.

At this time the Oakland side of the bay was a comparative wilderness, where cattle and wild animals roamed over the country, undisturbed. Only small crafts found their way across the bay and up the channel leading to the laguna, now called Lake Merritt. Near High Street, Alameda, an Indian rancheria stood on a mound. from which of recent date relics have been unearthed. The spot where the city now stands was covered with oak trees. Mexicans could be seen riding, with their serapes thrown around them, wearing on their heads high-crowned, broad-brimmed hats, their trousers or calyoneras were trimmed up the sides with fringe; while below the knees they wore leggins made of leather. Very large spurs of steel were clasped upon the heels of their boots, which they used upon the poor animals without mercy. Often the blood could be seen trickling from the flanks, also the mouths, of the horses. As a rule the bridle did not contain a brow-band, nor throat-latch. The strap of leather that held the bit in the mouth was one piece, slit enough at the ears to slip through to prevent the bridle from moving either way. The reins were strips of rawhide, plaited round. The bits consisted of a bar of iron on either side of the horses's jaw, about four inches in length, to the center of which was attached a bar or bit. To this a piece of iron was shaped to extend to the roof of the mouth. The reins were attached to the lower end of the bars, which extended on either side, about two inches below the horse's mouth; so that when the reins were pulled, the iron in the roof of the mouth acted as a lever to pry it open, being so severe that a slight touch of the reins would throw the mouth open.

The Mexicans often boasted of running their horses at full speed, and stopping them upon a bullock hide. This instrument of torture to the poor animals was very convenient for lassoing and handling stock. An incident related, occurred in Stockton early in the spring of 1849. The Jersey boys were getting ready to start to the mines. They were in the best of spirits, talking, singing and laughing, when some vaqueros rode up. In conversation with them, the Jersey boys had enquired about the use of such a severe bridle, which was explained. Having doubts in regard to the vaqueros stopping and turning so suddenly, one of them offered to bet fifty dollars that he could run fifty yards, turn around a stake, and get back to the starting point, before the vaquero with his horse. The Jersey man expected to be outstripped in going, but on returning, he thought he could turn the stake quicker than the horse, and consequently win. The wager was made. Horse and man toed the mark, starting at the drop of the hat. To the surprise of the bystanders, the horse was held back to run even with the man, until the stake was reached; then the horse was brought up and wheeled before the man could turn, coming out an easy winner.

The Mexican saddle had a high pommel in front, made very strong, upon which the riata was wound, to hold the animal when lassoed. The mochillas were two pieces of leather, two by two and a half feet in size, laced together and thrown over the saddle. About four inches from the front, the sides were cut to fit the pommel, and from this point laced, until the high back of the saddle was reached, where a slit was cut to fit over it. The mochilla was laced the same distance back of the saddle as in front of the pommel; both sides being embossed with showy figures. Tapideros made of leather covered the wooden stirrups in front and on the sides, which were stamped to match. The cinch was made of braided horse hair, fastened at each end to an iron ring, one end being fastened to the saddle. The Americans soon adopted the same method of cinching, as it was easier and safer. Nearly all the vaqueros had gay handkerchiefs wound about their heads under their hats. They never wore gloves, not even when attending a fandango.

Cattle were allowed to run at large all over the country. The time announced when each owner gathered his cattle, so that all cattlemen could be present. Vaqueros were sent out in all directions for a distance of ten miles or more, when they would camp the night previous to starting in the cattle. At an hour set early in the morning, each vaquero would run the cattle to a certain point, where they had been driven before and knew where to go, following in close pursuit. The cattle were crowded together upon the ground. Frequently there would be six or eight thousand head in a roundup. The Mexicans held the cattle by circling around them. The neighbor who found one with his brand drove it out from the bunch. A cow having a calf following her was driven home. The calf was marked and branded, then both were turned loose again.

Stock of every kind lived upon the old grass, which retained its nourishment until the first rains, in September or October, when the new grass appeared. Two or three weeks elapsed before it contained sufficient nutriment to keep the stock in a good condition. Very little barley or wheat was raised. Sometimes an acre or less was sown adjoining a vegetable garden.

The Mexicans were a hospitable people. Strangers arriving at any hour were received and entertained without charge. The Californians built their houses of adobe, covering the roof with tiles, and sometimes with tule. The partitions were also of adobe, and nearly always whitewashed. Sometimes there was a kind of plaster used, over which was pasted fancy paper, upon which was stamped the head of the devil, in the four corners of the room, near the ceiling; each face having a different fiendish expression. Castles with ivy-covered turrets were numerous. In the foreground, were scattered clusters of roses, and knights in full armor, riding their prancing steeds. The background was cream, or pale yellow in color. The dwellings were usually kept scrupulously neat.

The food of the Californians consisted of beef, frijoles, tortillas and vegetables. Frijoles, or beans cooked in the old Mexican style can not be equaled. They were seasoned with pepper and onions. After boiling all day, they were fried in fresh beef suet, or montego.

Both men and women of the lower element were very indolent. The men spent a great deal of time at the gambling table. Horse-racing and cock-fighting were their principal amusements. The women were exceedingly slothful. This class, of low instincts, intermarried with the Digger Indians.

Mexicans of the upper class were very aristocratic, priding themselves upon their lineage, which they could trace for generations back to the nobility of Spain. They were well educated, and married only equals in blood. Always dignified in carriage, the native costume gave them a distinguished air; notwithstanding, the senoritas manifested a preference for American husbands. With a few exceptions, the young ladies dressed in white during the four seasons, their shoes being tan color. They wore as a head covering, a scarf made of lace, or some dark material, thrown over the head, and crossed under the chin, each end falling down the back until almost reaching the ground.

The married women were usually attired in black, with a black, three-cornered shawl, heavily fringed, over their heads, and held under the chin with the left hand. When attending an evening entertainment, they were gorgeously gowned in silks and laces; their jewelry being of silver, set with diamonds, or turquoise and diamonds; also opals and diamonds.

DICKENSON HOUSE

Exploration of the Yosemite.

ON THAT MEMORABLE DAY, May 1st, 1846, when the emigrants were a short distance from Independence, they were overtaken by a young man about twenty-five years old, who remained with them several weeks. He was short in stature, having broad shoulders, light hair, and blue eyes; a social sort of man, full of fun and jokes. On the back of his coat was the word "Oregon," painted in large, red letters, which was his destination. One evening, after striking camp, he went to the stream and caught a number of frogs. When asked his object, he said they were delicious when fried in lard. They were cooked for his supper, which he seemed to enjoy, the others being too prejudiced to partake of them. This man was James Savage, discoverer of the Yosemite Valley.

After traveling over three hundred miles, he and a few of his company, turned towards Oregon; the Dickensons losing sight of him until after the discovery of gold, when they met him in the mines. He employed Indians to prospect for him, at the same time furnishing them with clothing, whiskey, and tobacco, balancing the articles sold with the gold he received. Learning to speak the Indian language from association, he became a favorite with the chief, whose daughter was offered him in marriage. Thinking the alliance would promote his interests as well as add to his safety, he accepted, and continued until he became the son-in-law of five chiefs. In a short time he had accumulated a large fortune, which he spent lavishly, never refusing assistance to those requiring help.

In 1850 the Yosemite tribe committed a great many depredations. They were enemies with the tribes into which Savage had married. The miners and stockmen organized a company and followed their trail, reaching the encampment about daylight, and taking them by surprise. About two hundred took refuge, no one knew where. Savage, who had won the title of Captain, compelled an Indian, who had been taken prisoner, to guide him to the hiding place of the Yosemites. He led him to the valley afterwards called Yosemite.

Captain Savage continued to live with the Indians until his death, which occurred in 1854, at Campbell's Ferry on Kings River, where he got into a dispute with Major Harvey about stock, knocking the Major down, who, when he arose, shot Savage dead. The report reaching the Indians that he had been shot, created intense excitement. Some went on foot, and others mounted their horses, hastening as fast as possible to the spot where Savage lay bleeding. Falling upon their knees, they sucked the blood from the wounds. It was a pitiful sight to witness their grief. Soon after Savage's death, his brother, Morgan Savage, arrived from Oregon to settle the estate, but found nothing available. No doubt Savage's influence kept the Indians under subjection. They were stupid creatures, but made good servants. The Mexicans often bought them from their parents as children, raising them as domestics.

In the autumn of 1854, a party visited Yosemite Valley, consisting of the following ladies and gentlemen: Mr. and Mrs. Calvin Cook, Mr. and Mrs. Samuel Miller, the Misses Mary and Anna Dallas, Mrs. A. G. Lawrey, J. J. and W. L. Dickenson. The above were the first American ladies to enter the valley. At that time, there was nothing but a trail to follow; consequently they were obliged to travel Indian-fashion, one after the other, on their horses. Often they came to narrow places in going around the mountain sides, where, had a horse missed his footing, he would have been precipitated hundreds of feet below. Pack animals were used to carry bedding, cooking utensils and provisions. On reaching the valley, they camped opposite Yosemite Falls, where their headquarters were established during their stay. A few Indians' wigwams were a short distance from camp. The Indians were friendly, supplying them with all the fish they required. Among them was an old squaw who attracted the party's attention on account of her aged appearance. When asked her age, one of them stated that she was one hundred and twenty years old.

Many have made an effort to describe Yosemite Valley, but all failed to impress one with its sublimity. Words are inadequate. One great artist, Hill, has spent years in studying the scenery of the valley. His paintings have brought fabulous prices; yet, you are not inspired with the same sense of awe upon beholding them. An English tourist, upon reaching Inspiration Point, was so struck with its grandeur that he could not utter a word. On his way down into the valley, he was asked how the scene impressed him. He expressed himself as feeling like dropping upon his knees and praying, although not a religious man. Many, upon first beholding it, shed tears.

LUELLA DICKENSON

Early Settlers.

THE EARLY EMIGRANTS were composed, principally, of men of intelligence and inflexible honesty; and women of perseverance and determination, combined with a sense of duty, which fitted them for the perilous journey across the plains. The majority were from the South and West. Many of the men had held prominent positions in their respective States. Among them was Benjamin S. Lippencott, who joined Fremont's battalion, serving as a Lieutenant until the close of the war. In the Constitutional Convention, he represented his district, and was twice elected to the State Senate, acquitting himself honorably.

Colonel Russell, another man deserving more than honorable mention, was Captain of a division that crossed the plains at the same time. He was well educated, intelligent and commanding in appearance; but could not write a legible hand. He was heard to say that, when the ink dried, he could not read his own handwriting. He became a successful politician.

Professor Grayson, the ornithologist, who was engaged in writing a book on ornithology at the time of his death, on the way over proved himself a good hunter and angler. During one of his excursions he found a beautiful piece of petrifaction, the grains of wood and bark being perfectly natural. One day he started off and did not return at the usual hour. The company was sure Indians had captured him. Next morning they pursued their journey, arriving about dusk at a deserted camp, where they found the Professor awaiting them, having spent the night with emigrants who had camped at this place. Mrs. Grayson had not manifested the least anxiety, being accustomed to her husband's venturesome habits. Their son, Edward, an infant at that time, after reaching manhood was drowned in the Pacific Ocean near an island where he had been engaged with his father in collecting specimens.

Among those who came across the plains in 1849, worthy of mention, was Judge Craven P. Hester, who with his family joined the missionary train; so called from all of its members being very religious, and having a number of ministers accompanying them. Night and morning prayers were always offered up, and the Sabbath kept holy by remaining in camp, and holding services during the day. Arriving in California late in the fall, they located near Sacramento, where they stayed until the excessive rains compelled them to leave the bottom lands. Many lost their household goods, barely escaping with their lives. The company disorganized, going to different points. The Hester family went to San Jose, where C. P. Hester was elected judge of the third district court, serving several terms. He bought a house that had been shipped around the Horn, and had it erected about a mile from San Jose on the Alameda where he resided until his death.

ACROSS THE PLAINS IN 1846

Our first Governor, Peter H. Burnett, was a firm man of strong character, and a writer of note. He crossed the plains to Oregon, coming from there to California, and selected San Jose as his home, where he remained until his children were educated, and some of them married. He then removed to San Francisco, soon afterwards being elected President of the Pacific Bank, a position he occupied until resigning in consequence of old age. His wife having died some time previous, he made his home with his eldest son, J. M. Burnett, where he died.

The Mormons who turned toward Salt Lake in 1846, reached their destination after many hardships. Finding little encouragement to settle there, Brigham Young sent a colony by a direct route to San Bernardino, where they were to make their headquarters, with the intention of eventually taking California; but the result of the war between the United States and Mexico forced them to change their plans.

1850 and 1851 were dry years. Scarcely any water ran in the creeks or gullies in the mountains, causing the dry diggings to be abandoned, and the mining to be confined to the river bottoms. Many of the miners were unable to meet their obligations; consequently the merchants failed, culminating in a general depression of all kinds of business throughout the State. Agriculture not being developed, the dependence rested upon the gold digger.

At this time a fire swept Stockton, reaching the Dickenson House, which was burned to the ground. The citizens, however, were an enterprising class, soon rebuilding with better material. The preceding year, a fire occurred in San Francisco, laying the city in ashes. In a short time, new buildings covered the burnt district. Another conflagration, more disastrous, happened soon after, when the people realized the necessity of erecting more substantial buildings. At this time a few brick kilns had been established, although not enough brick were burned to meet the demand, the deficit being shipped from the East. Stone was brought from China.

The first Legislature was held in San Jose, December 15, 1849. Among those encamped were two families from Missouri. Mary, the eldest daughter, was a beautiful young lady. Margaret, the eldest of the other family, attracted quite as much attention, and was soon engaged to a very wealthy man. One morning, while occupied in washing the breakfast dishes, she was seen to pick up the corner of her silk apron and wipe the frying pan. A lady present remarked, "Margaret, your apron will be spoiled;" when she retorted, "That is nothing; Josiah is rich."

The climate of Santa Clara Valley is noted for its salubrity. In the evening, when the sun was beginning to drop behind the Coast Range, the youths and maidens could be seen collecting in a corral near by, for the purpose of enjoying the sport of riding calves. Upon mounting, the calves would jump and plunge, frequently throwing the riders; but being young and active, they were on their feet again, and upon the calves' backs in the twinkling of an eye. Usually a large audience collected, adding zest to their merrymaking by clapping their hands. This may possibly meet the eyes of some of our prominent people who took part in the amusement.

The Mexicans afforded a great deal of amusement by their love of horse-racing. Almost every day vaqueros would assemble at the starting point. One would ride ahead and drop a hat, which the others were to pick up on their way to the turning spot, a few rods distant. To watch them make the turn and home-stretch was very exciting. Large sums were sometimes bet upon the result.

During the Legislature, a physician's wife, Mrs. B., accommodated a few of the members as a kindness, there being no desirable quarters. She was a very affable and witty woman, always ready to respond to a jest. Everybody liked to hear her talk, especially when she found her equal in wit to converse with. Some years afterwards, at a picnic, she met Mr. C. T. R., who had boarded with her. As usual, they began to spar at each other. The crowd gathered around, enjoying all that was said. For some time neither got the better of the other, until Mrs. B. intimated that Mr. R. was neglectful of his duty as a member of the Legislature. He responded, "I have always been a hard worker." She responded, "I know that you are a hard worker, especially when at the table. Your jaws were working all the time." All laughed immoderately. Mr. R., for the amusement of the bystanders and himself, asked Mrs. B. if he had not introduced and gotten through several important bills during his term, giving the title of each. "Yes," she replied, "I will admit all this to be true, and will go as far as to mention a title of one that you have overlooked, which was your favorite bill." "Will you be so kind as to give me the title of that bill?" "Certainly," she responded, "I can never forget it. It was the fill of fare." Here the conversation ceased and the crowd dispersed.

General Fremont.

J. C. FREMONT came to California in 1844. He started from Missouri, coming through Kansas, continuing westward over the Rocky Mountains, through the Great Basin, and crossed the Sierras not far from a beautiful lake, at that time not named, but afterwards called Lake Bigler, after General Bigler. His zeal for the Southern cause made him many enemies, through whose influence the name was changed to Lake Tahoe, after an Indian chief. In 1845, as Lieutenant-Colonel of a scientific expedition, J. C. Fremont returned to California, ostensibly for the purpose of seeking a nearer route. He was an ambitious man, gaining by his perseverance a reputation envied by many. He deserved more credit than he received, according to the opinion of Pioneers who were in his battalion during the war with Mexico. It is the misfortune of some, however, to pass through life, making sacrifices, and getting no credit. "There seems to be very little gratitude in this world," was the remark of a pessimist. A wit responded that he could not agree with him, as according to his opinion there was a great deal of gratitude in the world, as so little of it was used. The aggressiveness of men in high positions caused him many sleepless nights, and wore upon his constitution.

General Fremont married the daughter of Thomas H. Benton, United States Senator for thirty years from Missouri, and Elizabeth McDowell Benton, daughter of Governor James McDowell of Virginia, and Sarah Preston McDowell. Mrs. Fremont was a talented, graceful woman, and was the center of attraction wherever she appeared. Her family was opposed to her marriage. Mr. Benton tried to dissuade her from the step; but she was determined, telling him it was useless to try to break off the engagement, and that she would eventually marry him. At last Mr. Benton became quite angry and said if Charles came to see her again that he would give him h— —. His daughter had retained her calmness all through the conversation. When he made his remark, she placed her hand upon his arm, and looking him in the eyes, quietly remarked, "Father, had you not better change your mind and give him Jessie?"

John McDougal, Lieutenant-Governor at the time of Governor Burnett's resignation, was a talented men of fine prsence, a brilliant conversationalist, very affable, by profession a lawyer, and one of the best orators of that day. He was elected from Sacramento district to the Constitutional Convention of 1849. Being in favor of retrenchment, almost every question advanced by him was negatived. Yet, his honest convictions caused him to be elected Lieutenant-Governor by a great majority. He remained in San Jose several years with his family, then removed to San Francisco, where he died in 1866, having disappeared from public notice some time previous. Governor McDougal had one serious fault, that of imbibing too freely, finally losing control of his appetite, thereby becoming almost an imbecile.

James W. Manderville arrived in San Jose in the fall of 1849, having come to California for his health. He was at that time a young man of about twenty-three years of age. Limited in means he combined the practice of law with that of teaching. The house where he taught stood on the corner of First and Santa Clara Streets. an old adobe building covered with tile. His pupils were principally Americans. Through the winter the rain hardly ceased falling. All the adjacent streams were over their banks, and the streets were knee-deep in mud. Becoming discouraged, Mr. Manderville determined to go to the mines as soon as spring opened, thinking the climate more suitable and the chance of making money better. He located in Sonora, where he gained considerable reputation as a lawyer and politician, holding several important positions of trust. He placed William M. Gwin in nomination for United States Senator in 1857. A man of independent thought, generous and social, never aggressive in an argument, always meditating before coming to a conclusion, and firm in his opinion when his mind was fixed. No man had fewer enemies. He finally settled in San Francisco, where he died.

A typical old Irish gentleman by the name of Murphy, and his family, were among the first settlers. They came overland from Canada. His eldest son, James, bought a tract of land northeast of San Jose, where he lived to a good old age. The next son, Martin, settled upon a grant near Mountain View, where he brought up his family, educating his sons in Santa Clara College, with the exception of James, who graduated from St. Mary's College, San Francisco, and his daughters in the College of Notre Dame, San Jose. For Patrick,the eldest son, was purchased a grant of land in San Luis Obispo County, which was stocked with cattle and sheep, also a few hogs. Pat Murphy, as he was called by familiar friends, named his ranch Santa Margarita. The residence was unpretentious. However he entertained lavishly, maintaining bachelor's quarters for several years. At last he became a Benedict by marrying the daughter of Dr. O'Brien, a physician who had made a fortune in the mines, finding a resting place for his declining years on the Alameda, near Santa Clara, where he died. Miss O'Brien was a beautiful and accomplished young lady, having received her education at the College of Notre Dame, San Jose. Her musical attainments were the best. She was an exquisite performer upon the harp. Her graceful and suave manner made a charming picture. Mrs. Murphy died soon after marriage, and Mr. Murphy retired from public life for some time.

Upon resuming his position in politics, he was elected Senator from San Luis Obispo County, afterwards holding other offices of distinction. Senator Murphy took great pride in his Irish dialect, his ready wit being often the source of hilarious amusement. Senator Murphy was introduced to General Irwin McDowell in command of United States forces in San Francisco as Colonel Murphy. The General asked him if he was in the battle of Bull Run. Senator Murphy's reply was, "No, General, but I have made many a bull run." In politics, a Democrat; in person tall, and robust, until advanced in years, when the grippe placed its icy fingers upon him, terminating his career.

Martin, the second son, lost his life by the explosion of a steamboat, near Alviso. The third son, Bernard, studied law, following his profession until middle life, when he with others, established a bank in San Jose, of which he became president. Unfortunate investments caused a suspension of the bank, Bernard Murphy being a heavy loser. He was elected to the Assembly from Santa Clara County, having also held other responsible positions. He was one of the trustees of the Lick Estate. Longevity is an inheritance, and without accident, he will live for many years. Mr. Murphy married a young lady of San Francisco, who died at their home in San Jose recently, leaving a large and interesting family. James, the youngest son, was a talented man. He was appointed Bank Commissioner. Had not death claimed him at an early age he would have made himself a name. Elizabeth, the eldest daughter of Martin Murphy, is said to have been the first child of Anglo-Saxon parentage born in California. She married Mr. Taffe who died within a few years. Mrs. Taffe survived him only a short time. Mary Ann, the second daughter, graduated with the highest honors, and soon after married Mr. Richard Carroll of San Francisco, long since deceased. The youngest, Nellie, married Mr. Arquais, a descendant of one of the aristocratic Spanish families. Their residence is near Santa Clara.

The eldest Mr. Murphy, father of James, Martin, Dan, John and Mary Ann, settled near Gilroy, where he purchased a large grant, Murphy's Peak being named after him, and within his boundaries. Dan, his third son, married Miss Fisher. Her father was an Englishman and her mother a native of California. She received a large dowry at the time of her marriage, in land, cattle and sheep. John, lieutenant with Captain Weber in 1846, the fourth son, married Virginia Read, one of the sufferers of the Read and Donner party. She was a handsome young lady and was noted for her superior equestrianship, having obtained several first premiums at county fairs for her graceful riding. Lieutenant Murphy lost his eyesight some time before his death.

LUELLA DICKENSON

Mrs. Murphy led him to and from his office, performing the duties of an amanuensis. She gained, by experience, a sufficient knowledge of the real estate business to continue it after his death. Mary Ann, the only daughter, sister of James, Martin, Dan and John, married Captain Charles M. Weber. He built a residence in Stockton on the peninsula, of decided German architecture, not at all symmetrical, but roomy. The grounds were handsomely laid out. The cost of the residence was seventy-five thousand dollars. Captain Weber was considered an eccentric man. After living a retired life, Mrs. Weber died. Captain Weber ended his days in seclusion.

ACROSS THE PLAINS IN 1846

The Santa Clara Stage

IN 1850, SMALL STEAMBOATS plied between Alviso and San Francisco. To reach Alviso, people rode in a stage drawn by four mustangs, driven by an expert driver, who seemed well pleased when they reared and plunged, using a long whip with a cracker which excited the animals to a great extent. There was also a stage route by way of Santa Clara, Mayfield, Redwood City, Belmont, San Mateo and the old mission. This was better patronized, because it was quicker. The driver urged his horses to the top of their speed for a distance of ten or twelve miles, when a change was made, continuing to change horses at about the same distance, until reaching San Francisco. The road was full of ruts, and everybody received a dreadful shaking up before reaching his or her destination.

All kinds of traffic came and went over this route. Large wagons drawn by oxen, others by California horses, were loaded with merchandise. Next, a band of sheep driven by Mexican herders would appear. Following in their footsteps would likely be vaqueros driving a herd of cattle. The stage driver cautioned the occupants to be very quiet, and avoid making any demonstrations, as Spanish cattle were very wild and might attack and horn them to death. Observing the stage, the herd would stop, and the leaders tossing their heads, would knock their horns together, making a clinking sound, which caused the passengers to shiver, then, like a whirlwind, rush by filling the air with dust, almost to suffocation. The stage horses, being accustomed to cattle, did not move until spoken to by the driver.

Along this thoroughfare were people in private conveyances, people on foot, Mexicans riding burros, sometimes with a woman sitting on the same saddle in front of the man, invariably followed by two or more little Spanish curs. At that time, people were very enthusiastic, waving their hats as they would pass acquaintances; or in return for a salute from a stranger. Conventionalities seemed to be forgotten. Others, proved the mettle of their horses by racing with those who would take up the challenge, being followed by an excited throng, halloing at the top of their voices, and whipping their horses to keep in sight of the racers.

At one P.M. the passengers took dinner at the half-way house, twenty-five miles from San Jose, regaling themselves with California wine made from the mission grapes, a delicious beverage. After an hour's rest, the start would be made again. Everybody flocked out of the hotel to watch the stage depart. The driver would call,

LUELLA DICKENSON

"All aboard;" then there would be a rush and scramble for the seats. The first to reach the stage obtained the preferred seat at the side of the driver, who cracked his whip, and they were off. The horses would run for some distance before the driver could bring them to a trot. At the least provocation they would break into a gallop, and frequently into a run, before they could be checked. In this manner they continued until reaching San Francisco, where the coach arrived about 6 P.M.

DICKENSON HOUSE

ACROSS THE PLAINS IN 1846

"Mountain Charley"

EARLY ALL OLD CALIFORNIANS have heard of "Mountain Charley," who lived in the Santa Cruz mountains, where he hunted bear and deer. Some of his adventures were remarkable, especially the one recounted about meeting a grizzly that he fought without gloves. One morning quite early, he started out with his gun and had gone only a short distance, when he and the bear found themselves face to face. The grizzly was sitting on his haunches reaching for acorns when Charley came upon him. He tried to draw his gun, but, being at such close quarters, the bear disarmed him by striking the gun with its paw, knocking it out of his hands, at the same time embracing Charley. Both fell to the ground. Being on a hillside they rolled over and over, a distance of nearly one hundred feet, until they reached the ravine below, when the bear loosened his hold. They were then a few feet apart, the bear appearing to be more exhausted; yet did not seem inclined to give up the fight.

Charley realized that his only chance was to wind the bear by striking him with his fist over the heart. He landed a blow as near the region as possible, taking good care to stay very close to the bear, so that its claws would hang over him. He struck, first with one fist, then the other in rapid succession, when he found the bear weakening. By this time they were close to the embankment of the creek. The bear had lost no time in getting in his scratches and bites, having scratched Charley over the forehead, and down the cheek to the bone, tearing one eye from the socket. The bear had also fastened its teeth in "Mountain Charley's" left arm, making an ugly wound. With a desperate lunge he shoved the bear over the embankment into the water. Being too weak to stand, Charley fell prone upon the ground. The bear was in about the same condition. After lapping a little water, it waded to the opposite bank and lay down, occasionally looking in Charley's direction, who was perfectly still, as if dead.

At last the bear rose to his feet, walked up the steam, frequently stopping and looking back as if hesitating whether or not to renew the fight. Going at a slow pace it finally disappeared. When "Mountain Charley" thought he could move with safety, he crawled to the stream and sipped a little water, then washed the blood from his face, pushed the eye back into the socket, and crawled to his home. He was taken to San Jose for medical treatment. The surgeon found one of the bones of his forearm broken. Several months elapsed before he recovered. His eye was not destroyed, but his face was so disfigured his friends hardly knew him. Not at all discouraged by his experience, he continued to hunt until game became scarce, when he concluded to marry and settle down. Truly, love was blind in this instance.

Isaac Branham, a forty-niner, called "Uncle Ike" by all the young people who knew him, was another pioneer who was fond of hunting. He kept a pack of hounds. On moonlight nights and early in the morning their baying could be heard as they chased the coyote and coon. After a hunt, his friends were invited to his home to partake of bear steak and venison. His residence was about five miles from San Jose, on the road leading to the New Almaden quicksilver mines. He had planted a large orchard, and vineyard, from which there was a promise of handsome returns. Some of the land was covered with oak trees; the rest he sowed in grain.

Mr. Branham's family consisted of his wife, an amiable, loveable woman of marvelous energy. Although never strong, she always attended to her household duties with a cheerful smile upon her lips, imparting a feeling of welcome to her visitors. There were two sons and two daughters, Margaret, the elder daughter, married Mr. Osier, a wealthy farmer who lived north of San Jose on the Alviso road, where he owned a large tract of land, cultivating many acres to strawberries. Mr. and Mrs. Branham seemed happiest when they were surrounded by friends whom they entertained in an informal way.

Mr. Branham was a great admirer of fine stock. He raised a horse that for speed and endurance was superior to any in California at that time, naming him after his intimate friend, Benjamin Lippencott. He was a running horse, making his sixth mile in broken heats in 1:52, during the Santa Clara County Fair. He was a trim, beautiful animal, in color sorrel, and of Belmont stock.

Mr. and Mrs. Branham died at their home, within a short time of each other, esteemed by all who knew them. Their children are at present living in, or near, San Jose.

Samuel J. Hensley, who figured in the early history of California, was a major in the war with Mexico. He was an energetic man, engaging in different occupations in which he was successful, finally becoming the head of a steam navigation company, plying between San Francisco and Portland, Oregon; thus accumulating a large fortune. He married the daughter of Mr. Crosby, who was killed in a squatter's fight. He built a handsome residence in San Jose, situated on First Street, opposite that of Governor Burnett. His home consisted of a block of land with the house near the center, a few feet from the sidewalk. All kinds of ornamental shrubs and trees were planted.

Major and Mrs. Hensley experienced the sorrow of having several children die at an early age, being interred beneath a bower of rose vines in their garden. Two children lived to be grown, Charles and Ella. Charles married, and settled near Napa, where he died. Ella married Mr. Thornton, son of Judge Thornton, and is at present living in San Francisco.

The Major was a tall, spare man, with sharp features, and a benign countenance. When at home he took great pleasure in entertaining his friends at cards, euchre being his favorite game, and at that time quite fashionable. It was said that W. T. Wallace, John H. Moore, Austin Thompson and the Major often met to play poker, the stakes sometimes reaching ten thousand dollars. Major Hensley died some time in the early sixties, leaving many warm friends. His wife still survives him.

Josiah Belden, a solid, well educated man of pleasant address, made his money in the mines, investing it in San Francisco, and City of Mexico property; also New York. He purchased a piece of land adjoining Governor Burnett's home, building a fine residence where he took his bride, Margaret Jones, the daughter of very pious parents. She was brought up in the Presbyterian Church, always adhering to the doctrine, and is a very conscientious woman, beloved by all who know her. Soon after the Civil War, Mr. and Mrs. Belden, with their family, removed to New York, where he died recently. Mrs. Belden will no doubt spend the remaining years of her life in the home her husband established in New York.

LUELLA DICKENSON

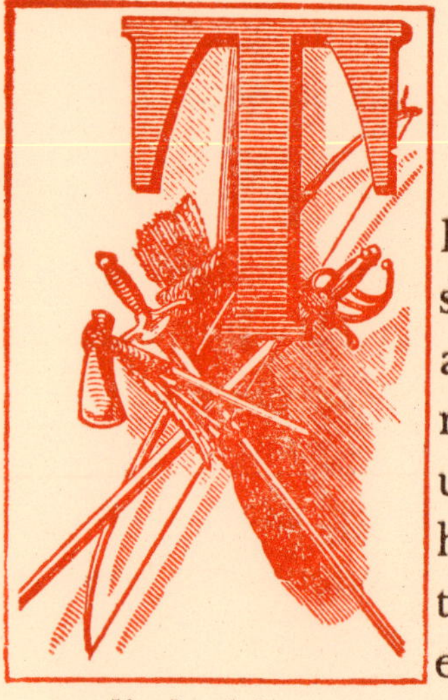

HERE CAME FROM MISSOURI to San Jose a youth hardly sixteen years of age, who was determined to make a living at anything honorable. It could be discerned that he had been reared in refinement. He performed chores and swept offices until saving enough money with which to buy a horse and cart, he went from house to house soliciting the privilege of keeping their yards clean, at a price set. In this way he soon accumulated enough to go to the mines, where he met with success. He then studied with a private teacher, finishing his education and becoming one of the most polished young men of the day. Hardly any gathering was considered complete unless Drury Malone was there. Being an inveterate talker, his voice could be heard above the clamor of conversation. He entered the political field, and was honored with several important offices. He was twice married, his second wife being Miss Woodward, daughter of the owner of Woodward's Gardens. Soon after his marriage he purchased a country home in Napa County, naming it Oak Knoll, where he spent the summer with his family, residing with them at the Palace Hotel during the winter season. His son, a very promising youth, died suddenly. Mr. Malone could not reconcile himself to his death, and only survived him a short time.

C. T. Ryland, a member of one of the old Southern families, came to California when a young man. Gifted with more than ordinary intellect, he was soon a leading lawyer in San Jose. He married Letitia, the eldest daughter of Governor P.H. Burnett. Mr. Ryland led an exemplary life, and although accumulating great wealth, was never ostentatious. He was elected to the Assembly by the Democrats in 1855. During the Civil War, he was a staunch Union man, but after peace was declared, he returned to the Democratic party. He died after a lingering illness at his home, leaving a large family, and many friends to regret his loss. Mrs. Ryland is living in the old home, surrounded by several of her children who have remained unmarried.

W.T. Wallace was born in Kentucky. His grandfather, on his father's side, was a Presbyterian minister, and graduate of Princeton College. Being an eloquent preacher, he filled his pulpits most acceptably. He was one of the pioneer ministers of Kentucky. William T. Wallace at the age of sixteen, concluding his education was sufficient to carry him through the world, left his home, following his uncle, Major Roman, through the war with Mexico; this adventurous kind of life being to his liking.

ACROSS THE PLAINS IN 1846

The Major was a college graduate, and linguist, and well prepared to teach his nephew how to shoot. Encouraged by having the best material to work with, as soon as peace was declared Major Roman took upon himself the task of completing W. T. Wallace's education, which was accomplished in a short time, when he took up the study of law. Immediately after finishing his course he entered into co-partnership with C. T. Ryland in San Jose. He married Romie, the second daughter of Governor P. H. Burnett, purchasing a residence on First Street, between Santa Clara and San Fernando streets, now the heart of the city; all trace of the home now being blotted out by brick buildings.

About the year 1870 W. T. Wallace removed with his family to San Francisco. From the time he entered public life to the present time he has been considered one of the most talented men in California. After holding several positions of trust, he received the appointment of Chief Justice, serving out his term. Judge and Mrs. Wallace had the misfortune of losing three children after reaching their majority. Four children are left to console them, two sons and two daughters, all married and living in San Francisco. Judge and Mrs. Wallace occupy their residence on Van Ness Avenue.

James Montgomery from Kentucky crossed the plains, reaching Monterey in 1847. He was a descendant of the noted Montgomerys of New Jersey, his grandfather having gone through the wilderness to Kentucky about the year 1781. June, 1848, Mr. Montgomery went to the mines, obtaining enough gold to enable him to return to Kentucky, where he bought the finest horses and cattle that could be found, driving them across the plains to a point in San Joaquin valley, on Bear Creek, which he had selected for pasturage. There were only a few settlements in the valley at that time, and those were along the streams, making the range extensive. He remained in the business for many years, accumulating a large fortune. He suffered greatly by the drought in 1864, which destroyed half the stock in California. At that date no provisions were made for feeding the herds, the only resort being to drive them to the mountains where they could browse.

Mr. Montgomery, by his energy, had regained his losses to some extent, when the land excitement broke out. The land having been thrown upon the market by the government, was all bought up, and divided into farms, compelling the stock men to abandon the business, and force the stock upon the market, which ruined a great many. Mr. Montgomery took a philsophical view of the condition, taking his losses as a natural consequence. Afterwards, while riding on the cars with a friend, through the valley where his cattle by thousands had grazed, he saw the country covered with fields of grain, handsome homes, and cities built where the cattlemen had rounded up their cattle. After meditating a while, his friend remarked, "Mr. Montgomery, if you had sold your cattle for thirty dollars per head, and bought this land at a dollar and a quarter an acre, you would now be a very rich man." Mr. Montgomery replied in a slow and easy way, "Yes, that is so, but it requires a man of d— little intelligence to tell that now."

Mr. Montgomery was elected to the Senate from Merced and Stanilaus Counties. He married in Independence, Missouri, when returning to California after purchasing stock. His brother, Warren Montgomery, was elected from the same counties, previous to his election, being the youngest man ever elected to the Senate in California, and likely the youngest in any of the States of the Union, having scarcely reached his majority.

A ball was once given by Thomas O. Larkin, United States Consul at Monterey. Among those who attended were General Sherman, Captain Naglee, Tolbert H. Green, Stephen A. Wright, wife and daughter, Dr. Isbell and wife, Joseph Curtis, Sheriff Winn, James Gardner and wife, Mr. and Mrs. Taber, Miss Mary Taber and Mr. Angel (after whom Angels Camp and Angels Creek were named, he having been the first settler at that place), Mr. Temple and Captain Andros Pico, (brother of Governor Pio Pico), and wife. They were the parents of Captain Romaldo Jose Pico who was in the service of the United States against the Indians during the Civil War. There were also present some members of the Vallejo family. Col. Sinol, wife and daughter, Sinol, Jr., Supelveda, William F. Swasey, Lieutenant Ord, and many others whose names cannot be recalled. The ball took place in a hall used for all kinds of entertainments, being lighted with fish oil lamps. As a compliment, as well as for the entertainment of his guests, Mr. Larkin invited the Spanish guests to execute some of their native dances. The figures in one, resembled to a great extent those of the german. The music was played upon stringed instruments by Mexicans, in quick, sparkling time. The senor, dressed in Spanish costume, made of black velvet, trimmed with gilt braid and fringe, advanced hat in hand, until reaching a lady on the opposite side of the room, he clapped his hands, at the same time making a low bow; then receded to the center of the room, followed by the lady, who, upon reaching the center, executed a few intricate steps, ending in a whirl. The same figure was repeated until all engaged in the dance had been on the floor.

The next was the Spanish dance with castanets, danced by a young lady in a bright red dress above her shoe tops, her movements being exceedingly graceful. Refreshments were served at intervals, the ball continuing until daylight, when the adios were spoken, and all departed.